Let's Go To London
Copyright © Alex Moss & Selina Moss
Wonder Wide Publishing, 2024

Hi! I'm Wilber from Wonder Wide. I've visited every page in this book (even this one). Can you find me?

Claim Your FREE Activity Book. Scan Me >>

LET'S GO TO...
LONDON

Hello Explorer!

Welcome to your fun-filled guide to London! Are you ready to uncover the secrets of a city where history hides around every corner? Fasten your seatbelt because we're off to London, a city of ancient castles and modern wonders.

This isn't just a book; it's your ticket to a world of fun, mystery, and adventure. Inside, you'll discover amazing facts about London, from the top of the Shard to the depths of the London Underground. You'll visit the homes of kings and queens, discover where dinosaurs live, and even learn about the hidden prison inside Big Ben.

But hold on, there's more! This book is also filled with puzzles, colouring pages, and lots of fun activities that will make your journey through London even more exciting. You'll try to find your way out of a maze, design your own landmark, and even get a bus to jump over Tower Bridge!

In London, every cobblestone street has a tale to tell, and every new place is an adventure waiting to happen. So, pack your imagination and get ready for the journey of a lifetime. London is waiting for you, let's go explore!

P.S. If you need an activity answer, ask an adult to scan the special code on the last page.

Wilber

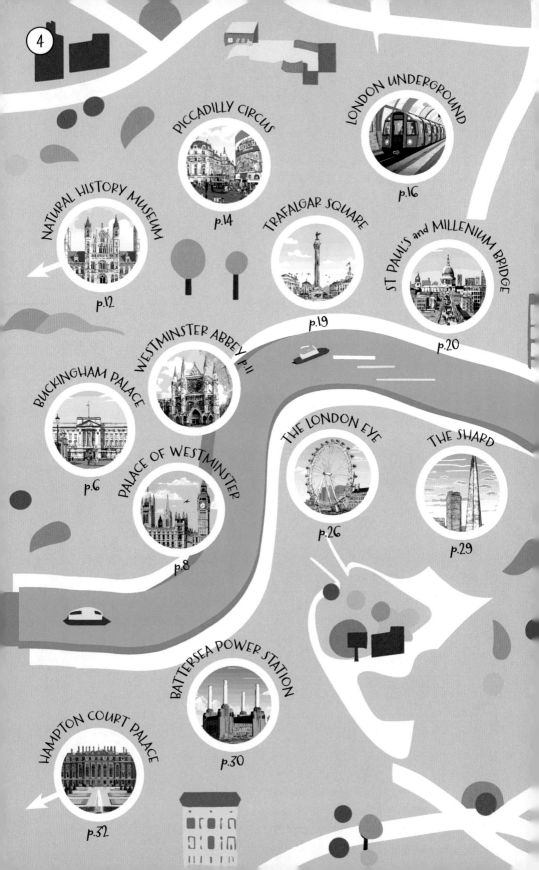

4

PICCADILLY CIRCUS
p.14

LONDON UNDERGROUND
p.16

NATURAL HISTORY MUSEUM
p.12

TRAFALGAR SQUARE
p.19

ST PAUL'S and MILLENIUM BRIDGE
p.20

WESTMINSTER ABBEY p.11

BUCKINGHAM PALACE
p.6

THE LONDON EYE
p.26

THE SHARD
p.29

PALACE OF WESTMINSTER
p.8

BATTERSEA POWER STATION
p.30

HAMPTON COURT PALACE
p.32

THE MONUMENT p.22

THE TOWER OF LONDON p.42

RIVER THAMES AND BARRIER p.40

TOWER BRIDGE p.44

MILLENIUM DOME p.39

THE GLOBE THEATRE p.24

CUTTY SARK p.36

THE ROYAL OBSERVATORY p.34

BUCKINGHAM PALACE

Buckingham Palace has 775 rooms but started life much smaller as 'Buckingham House'. This town house was built for the Duke of Buckingham in 1703, over 300 years ago. It didn't become the main Royal home until Queen Victoria came to the throne.

If the King is in, the Royal Standard flag will be flying. If he's out, the Union flag will be flying.

The Victoria Memorial is a monument to Queen Victoria. She reigned for 63 years between 1837 — 1901.

Buckingham Palace sits at the end of a famous road called The Mall. It begins at Trafalgar Square via Admiralty Arch. The surface of The Mall is coloured red to make it look like a giant red carpet leading up to Buckingham Palace! The Palace is guarded by real soldiers who wear famous bearskin hats and red tunics. You can watch the Changing of the Guard ceremony outside the Palace. The soldiers on duty, called the Old Guard, change places with the New Guard.

Here is a Palace Guard in his bearskin hat and red tunic.
Can you spot 11 differences between the two pictures?

There are over 1000 rooms in the Houses of Parliament!
Can you find your way from one end to the other?

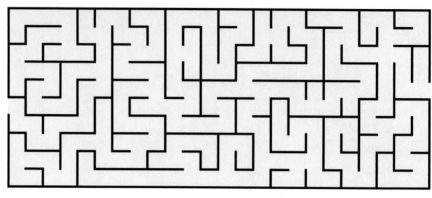

On November 5th 1605,
Guy Fawkes tried to blow up the
Houses of Parliament, known as
the Gunpowder Plot. Every year
people in the UK celebrate Bonfire
Night with fireworks to remember
this event.

In the early days of Parliament,
people brought swords with them.
Today, there are still places to
hang a sword, but it's just tradition
now. Many rooms still have
marks two sword lengths apart,
to stop fights between people who
disagreed with each other!

Sitting on the north side of the River Thames, the Palace
of Westminster dates back over 900 years. It was once home to
Kings and Queens. It's now home to the Government and known
as the Houses of Parliament where laws are made. It has over
1000 rooms. In 1834 two workmen were ordered to burn all the
'tally sticks', an old way of counting money using pieces of carved
wood. It caused a fire that completely destroyed the palace.

THE PALACE OF WESTMINSTER

BIG BEN AND THE HOUSES OF PARLIAMENT

Big Ben has lost its colour! Can you help put it back?

One New Year's Eve the clock slowed due to heavy snow and ice on the hands. The New Year was chimed-in nine minutes late.

Most people know this famous clock tower as 'Big Ben'. Originally called the Clock Tower, it was renamed the Elizabeth Tower for Queen Elizabeth II's Diamond Jubilee. Big Ben is the nickname of the Great Bell of the clock; it weighs about the same as two elephants. Inside the tower is a secret prison room, although it hasn't been used for over 100 years.

A special window was made in Westminster Abbey to celebrate the longest-reigning monarch in British history, Elizabeth II. Called The Queen's Window, it has vibrant colours and was created by the famous artist, David Hockney.

Create your own brightly coloured stained glass window.

Can you spot 7 differences between these two stained glass windows?

WESTMINSTER ABBEY

The Abbey has been the official coronation church for British Kings and Queens since William the Conqueror in 1066. There is a special chair in the Abbey, known as the Coronation Chair, where every King or Queen has been crowned since 1308.

Westminster Abbey is over 1000 years old and originally built on an island in the Thames called Thorney Island. It has the oldest door in England, also around 1,000 years old. It's made from a single tree that may have started life another 500 years before that!

Unlike most abbeys, it doesn't belong to the Church of England. It's called a 'Royal Peculiar' because it belongs to the sovereign (King or Queen).

NATURAL HISTORY MUSEUM

The museum's founder and world-famous naturalist, Sir Richard Owen, invented the word 'dinosaur'. Before he did, people just called them dragons!

The museum is famous for its dinosaur skeletons. The central 'Hintze Hall' used to contain 'Dippy', the diplodocus but now a blue whale skeleton 'Hope' lives there. You can walk right underneath the largest creature ever to have lived.

When you're in the Hintze Hall where 'Hope' the blue whale is, look up and see the monkeys climbing the arches of the ceiling and woodland creatures cuddling in the corner columns.

The Natural History Museum opened in 1881 nearly 150 years ago. That might seem old, but some of the fossils inside are 500 million years old! This beautiful building contains over 80 million items from different parts of the natural world and is often called the 'Cathedral of Nature'. The Natural History Museum is one of three big museums on Exhibition Road including the Science Museum and Victoria and Albert Museum.

DIPPY

HOPE

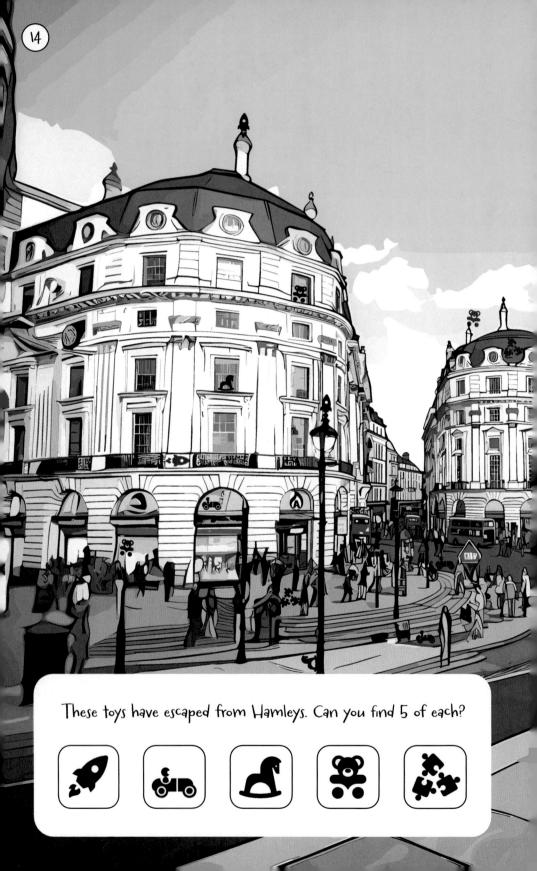

These toys have escaped from Hamleys. Can you find 5 of each?

PICCADILLY CIRCUS

Piccadilly Circus is known for its bright advertising boards. They are one of the most famous sights in London, and they have been shining brightly for over 100 years!

Just a short walk from Piccadilly Circus, you'll find Regent Street. It's famous for its shops, including Hamleys, the oldest toy shop in the world!

Despite its name, Piccadilly Circus is not a place where you'll find acrobats or clowns. The word 'circus' comes from 'circle', because it was once a complete roundabout. That changed when the heart of London's West End theatre district, Shaftsbury Avenue, was built but the name stuck! Near Piccadilly Circus is the Ritz hotel. It's one of the fanciest hotels in the world and famous for its afternoon tea.

LONDON UNDERGROUND

Every week, the London Underground escalators travel the equivalent distance of going twice around the world.

The London Underground, also known as the Tube, is the oldest subway system in the world. It started running way back in 1863. More than half the 249-mile network is not actually underground but runs above the surface!

When the Underground was first built, the trains had no windows, as the engineers thought there was nothing for passengers to see!

The shortest distance between two stations is on the Piccadilly line. It's only 260 metres between Covent Garden and Leicester Square and takes less than 30 seconds. It's probably quicker to walk between them than get the Tube!

There are 272 stations on the London Underground, but only about 30 of them are south of the River Thames. There are also around 40 abandoned stations!

Can you complete the word search challenge?
Find all 12 London Underground stations.

```
M E L C E E R I W Q F Z D K X U L K
O V U H U I V A B Y C M O G P J U J
N W R S I U A I K O G W C Y O Z E B
U L D O T G U H C D N X F R P G W R
M I F A T O H N A T Q M C L L P M I
E T I V L I N G Z D O L P G A I Z X
N H E B U D H B A B P R A V R M N T
T R O M F U G G U T A Z I K Z L N O
Q G U G P O H A C E E N V A D I O N
W A T E R L O O T W H R K J E C G G
S H T G B I E T I E V J R F U O E L
S A B X C Y L A N G E L Y G A K S I
```

- [ ] ALDGATE
- [ ] ANGEL
- [ ] BANK
- [ ] BRIXTON
- [ ] EUSTON
- [ ] HIGHGATE
- [ ] PIMLICO
- [ ] MONUMENT
- [ ] POPLAR
- [ ] TEMPLE
- [ ] WATERLOO
- [ ] VICTORIA

The Underground can feel like a maze! Can you find
your way from the train to the exit?

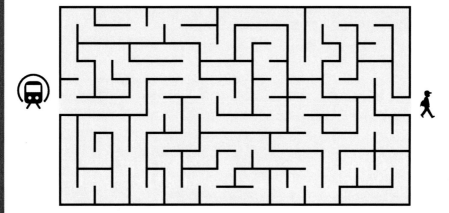

Complete and Colour HMS Victory

HMS Victory was Lord Nelson's ship at the Battle of Trafalgar.

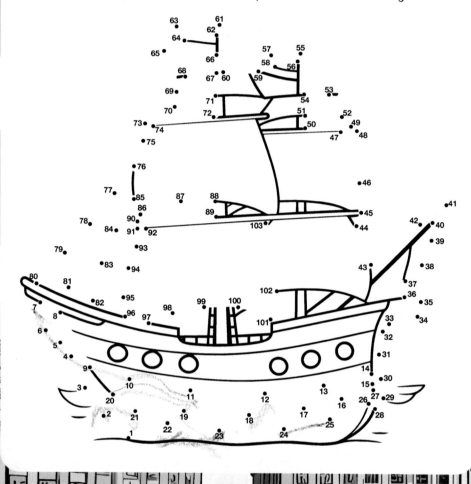

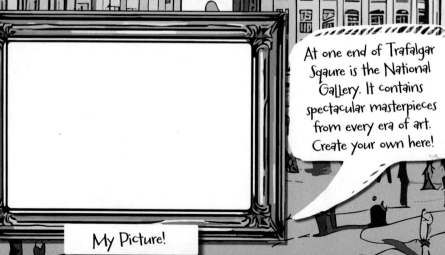

At one end of Trafalgar Sqaure is the National Gallery. It contains spectacular masterpieces from every era of art. Create your own here!

My Picture!

TRAFALGAR SQUARE

Towering over Trafalgar Square is Admiral Lord Nelson, one of England's greatest heroes. He joined the Navy aged 12 and went on to win many battles at sea. He died during his most famous victory over the French and Spanish Navy, at the battle of Trafalgar.

Just south of Trafalgar Square on a small roundabout is the statue of King Charles I. It's the place where all distances to London are measured from. Look for the plaque on the floor that tells you about it.

Four huge bronze lions surround the column, and each one is slightly different. They are known as the Landseer lions, after their creator Sir Edwin Landseer. Each lion weighs as much as three family cars. It's said that if Big Ben ever chimes 13 times, they will come alive!

Bronze panels on each side have pictures of Nelson's battles. They were made from French guns that were captured and melted down.

ST PAUL'S CATHEDRAL
AND THE MILLENNIUM BRIDGE

Look up at the two towers and see the golden pineapples! In the past, they were a sign of welcome and hospitality.

Inside the dome, there's a Whispering Gallery. Whisper against the walls and someone on the other side of the room 30 metres away can hear you!

St Paul's Cathedral has been destroyed four times in its history. It was last rebuilt after the Great Fire of London over 300 years ago. Designed by famous architect Sir Christopher Wren, it was once the tallest building in London. The dome is 365 feet high, about the same as 25 double-decker London buses. You can climb 528 steps to the Golden Gallery for amazing views. Many important people are buried at St. Paul's, including its architect Sir Christopher Wren and Lord Nelson.

Who whispered that?

Can you work out where whispered came from? Trace it back to the right person and write the word in the box.

JELLY

BRIDGE

FUNNY

This footbridge was named the Millennium Bridge because it was opened in the year 2000. It quickly became known as the 'Wobbly Bridge' as it began to sway frighteningly when people walked over it. It closed after just one day and took two years to fix. The Millennium Bridge has appeared in several films and TV shows, with the most famous probably being "Harry Potter and the Half-Blood Prince", where it collapses.

THE MONUMENT
TO THE GREAT FIRE OF LONDON

On top of The Monument is a golden ball of fire. It's there to remind us of the Great Fire. If you want to get to the top of The Monument, you have to climb up 311 steps.

Most of London's buildings were made from wood and built close together. With few ways to tackle fires in those days, the blaze raged for four days, spread by strong winds. It destroyed over 13,000 houses and nearly 100 churches.

The Monument was built to remember the Great Fire of London in 1666 that burned down much of the city. The Monument is 202 feet tall, which is exactly the distance from its base to the bakery of Thomas Farriner on Pudding Lane where the Great Fire started. Hidden beneath The Monument is a tiny laboratory made for scientific experiments. It was quickly abandoned as the surrounding area was too busy.

Draw your own picture of the Great Fire of London.

A man called Samuel Pepys wrote a famous diary about what happened during the Great Fire of London. Find his hidden message by searching for each flame and the secret letter it contains. Come back and write the letter in to the correct flame. Then, unscramble the letters to make a word.

Tower of London (p.44)

St Paul's Cathedral (p.20)

Piccadilly Circus (p.14)

Cutty Sark (p.36)

London Underground (p.16)

Unscramble the letters here.

THE GLOBE THEATRE

The Globe Theatre is the only building in London allowed to have a thatched roof, made of materials like straw. After the Great Fire of London in 1666, thatched roofs were banned because they can catch fire easily.

The theatre is open-air, which means there's no roof over the stage or the yard. So, if it rains, the actors get wet!

The Globe Theatre is where William Shakespeare's plays were performed. He was a famous English playwright, poet and actor. He lived over 400 years ago and wrote stories like "Romeo and Juliet" and "Much Ado About Nothing". The first Globe Theatre was built over 400 years ago but burned down during a performance when a special effect with a cannon set the roof on fire! The new Globe Theatre is just like the original, but only about 30 years old.

MUCH ADO ABOUT NOTHING
BY WILLIAM SHAKESPEARE

Once upon a time in a town called Messina, there were two brave soldiers, Claudio and Benedick, who came back from a great battle. Claudio fell in love with a girl named Hero, and they wanted to get married.

But a devious person named Don John made up a story to make Claudio think that Hero was not being honest. This made Claudio sad, and he didn't want to marry Hero anymore.

Meanwhile two friends, Beatrice and Benedick, always teased each other. However, secretly they liked one another, even if they didn't want to admit it. Their friends thought it would be funny to make them each believe they loved each other secretly.

In the end, all the misunderstandings were cleared up. Claudio and Hero realised they truly loved each other and got married. Beatrice and Benedick also admitted their love and decided to get married. Don John's mean tricks didn't work, and everyone had a big celebration.

And so, in Messina, they discovered that love and honesty always win in the end.

Can you find 5 hidden roses on this page?

LONDON EYE

The London Eye has 32 capsules, thought to represent each of London's 32 boroughs. However, they are numbered from 1 to 33 because some people think 13 is an unlucky number! It can carry 800 people at a time, the same as 11 double-decker London buses.

Just like the Eiffel Tower in Paris, the London Eye was only supposed to be there for a short time, around five years. However, it's still one of the most popular attractions in the UK. On a clear day you can see as far as Windsor Castle 25 miles away.

A ride on the London Eye takes about 30 minutes. It moves slowly so you can get on and off without it stopping.

Can you match the 6 pairs?

A.
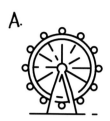

B.
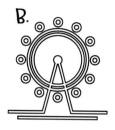

C.
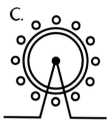

D.
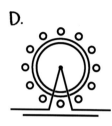

E.
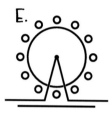

F.
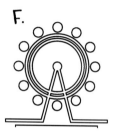

G.
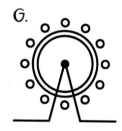

H.
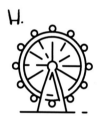

I.
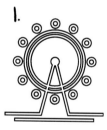

J.
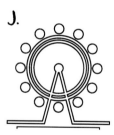

K.
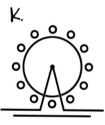

L.
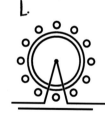

Write your answers here...

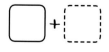

Complete and Colour Romeo the fox.

ROMEO

THE SHARD

Although it's tall, the world's tallest building, the Burj Khalifa in Dubai, is nearly three times higher!

During construction a fox moved into the Shard and lived at the top. Known as Romeo, he lived off the scraps of food left by builders.

The Shard is the tallest building in the UK and in Western Europe. It has 11,000 glass panels on the outside. Sitting close to London Bridge Station on the south bank of the River Thames, from the top you can see for 40 miles on a clear day. Architect Renzo Piano first sketched the design on a restaurant napkin. Originally called 'London Bridge Tower', the Shard got its name from critics who didn't like the design. They called it "a shard of glass through the heart of historic London." Renzo loved it, and the name was born!

BATTERSEA POWER STATION

The power station was designed by Sir Giles Gilbert Scott who also designed the red telephone box, another famous British icon.

Battersea Power Station was a huge coal-fired power station. Today, it's a place where people live, shop, and have fun. It's one of the largest brick buildings in the world, made up of around 61 million bricks. Battersea is famous for its four huge chimneys, each twice as wide as a London Underground tunnel. However, the building is really two power stations connected together, each with two chimneys. Battersea 'A' was built first but Battersea 'B' wasn't completed until 20 years later, creating the iconic four-chimney structure.

Can you complete the word search challenge?
Find the 12 different energy resources?

```
I  K  S  K  E  L  H  Q  X  K  N  U  C  L  E  A  R  K
W  B  R  H  T  L  C  Y  C  J  K  Y  U  E  H  Q  G  R
B  I  T  Y  S  H  O  T  D  T  L  I  V  U  U  E  E  K
O  O  X  D  O  G  A  S  U  R  F  W  X  B  J  K  O  T
S  M  L  R  L  K  L  O  J  Q  O  E  W  U  R  O  T  I
V  A  S  O  A  P  C  N  M  D  O  P  A  D  W  E  H  D
G  S  N  G  R  V  G  O  R  O  H  W  O  K  U  L  E  A
X  S  P  E  T  Z  A  T  I  A  S  T  Y  W  Y  X  R  L
A  Q  P  N  A  P  Q  G  E  L  T  W  A  V  E  F  M  H
A  N  M  F  Y  S  A  K  J  Q  H  O  B  N  D  R  A  W
Y  D  U  H  D  C  I  Z  X  Q  I  W  I  N  D  I  L  F
U  Z  H  Z  B  U  X  A  P  X  W  W  Q  X  R  V  C  M
```

- ☐ OIL
- ☐ COAL
- ☐ GAS
- ☐ HYDROPOWER
- ☐ SOLAR
- ☐ BIOMASS
- ☐ WIND
- ☐ GEOTHERMAL
- ☐ WAVE
- ☐ TIDAL
- ☐ NUCLEAR
- ☐ HYDROGEN

Can you connect the old power lines at Battersea? Draw power lines to connect the same coloured dots together. Only one power line can be in any square. They can't cross over, touch or go diagonally.

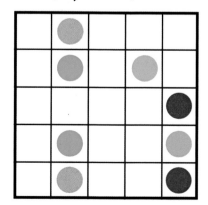

Take a look at this example to help you.

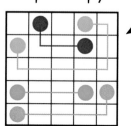

HAMPTON COURT PALACE

Hampton Court Palace has the oldest hedge maze in Britain. Its tall hedges are over 300 years old. It's easy to get lost, but that's part of the fun!

The 500-year-old tennis court at the palace is one of the oldest sports venues in the world.

Hampton Court Palace is best known as the home of King Henry VIII. He was famous for having six wives in his lifetime. Henry loved eating and installed kitchens with 200 cooks that could serve meals for 800 people, twice a day! It also had a special kitchen just for making chocolate. When his only son Edward was born, Henry ordered spectacular tapestries to celebrate. These woven artworks were made with cloth of gold with each tapestry costing the price of a warship.

Can you make your way through the Maze at Hampton Court Palace?

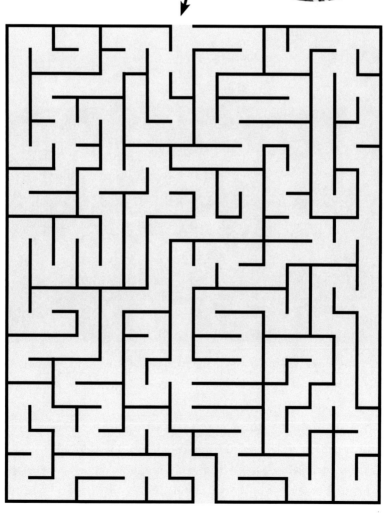

THE ROYAL OBSERVATORY

A bright red Time Ball on top of the building drops at exactly 1 p.m. every day. It was the first public time signal in the country. It could be seen by ships on the Thames and allowed them to set their time accurately before heading out to sea.

The Royal Observatory sits at the top of a hill in Greenwich Park where a castle once stood. It is where "Greenwich Mean Time" (GMT) comes from, the centre of world time. It looks down over the Maritime Museum, which was once a palace where Henry VIII was born. A line on the ground at the observatory is called the Prime Meridian. This marks the dividing line between the eastern hemisphere (most of Africa, Europe, Asia, and Australia) and the western hemisphere (includes North and South America). If you stand on it, you're standing in both hemispheres at the same time!

What has been your favourite thing about London so far?
Or what are you most looking forward to? Write about it here...

_____

_____

_____

_____

_____

_____

_____

_____

_____

_____

_____

_____

_____

_____

_____

_____

CUTTY SARK

The Cutty Sark is a famous ship that carried tea from China to England. Built in Scotland over 150 years ago, it was one of the last 'tea clipper' ships ever made.

When the Cutty Sark had all its sails out, they would cover an area half the size of a football pitch.

In its day, it was one of the fastest ships on the sea. It held the record for the fastest journey from England to Australia for ten years.

In 2007 the Cutty Sark caught fire and burned for several hours. Having been closed for repairs, thankfully about half of the ship's materials had been removed and stored elsewhere. The fire was believed to have been caused by a vacuum cleaner that was left on.

The Cutty Sark tea crate challenge!

Finish loading these crates of tea on to the Cutty Sark in the correct order. The crates can only go next to each other if they have the same numbered spot. Draw the spots on the correct crate.

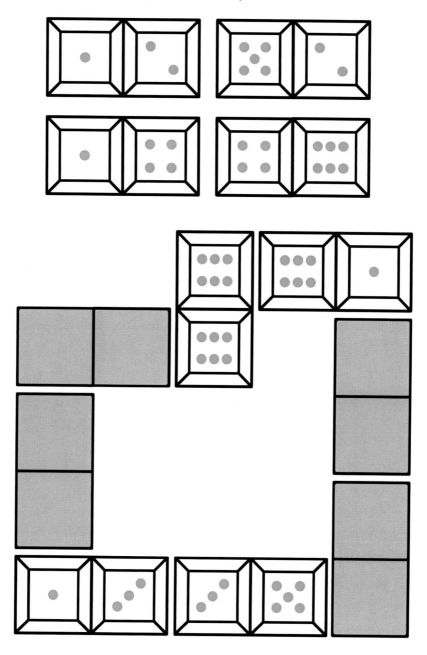

Design your own amazing landmark.

London is full of incredible buildings, here's a chance to design your own!

Here are some of London's famous landmarks to give you inspiration.

Nelson's Column   London Eye   Tower Bridge

Tower of London   The Dome   The Shard

MILLENNIUM DOME

The Millennium Dome, now known as The O2, is the largest dome structure in the world. It's high enough to fit the Statue of Liberty inside. It was originally built to celebrate the start of the new millennium in the year 2000.

The dome is now an entertainment complex and concert arena, with shops, cinemas and two music venues. A walkway across the top of the dome allows visitors to cross the roof!

The design was inspired by time and the Greenwich Meridian Line that passes just next to it. There are 12 yellow towers that hold up the roof, one to represent each month of the year. The roof is 52 metres high in the middle, one metre for each week of the year. The dome is 365 metres wide, one metre for every day of the year. Finally, there are 24 arches around the base, for each hour of the day.

THE RIVER THAMES
AND THE THAMES BARRIER

In 1251, King Henry III was given a polar bear as a present by the King of Norway. It was kept at the Tower of London. The bear was allowed to swim and hunt for fish in the Thames!

In the past, when the winters were much colder than today, the Thames would freeze over. People held 'frost fairs' on the ice with food stalls, games and ice-skating!

The River Thames runs through the heart of London. At 215 miles, it's the longest river in England and the second longest in the United Kingdom. It's home to 125 different types of fish and even a whale was once spotted! The Thames Path is 184 miles long, which makes it the longest river walk in Europe. The part of the river that flows through London is tidal. That means it changes direction and goes out to the sea then comes back in twice a day. To protect London from flooding, the Thames Barrier was built. It creates a solid steel wall that stops water from flowing upstream toward the city. It's the second largest flood barrier in the world.

Draw your own polar bear

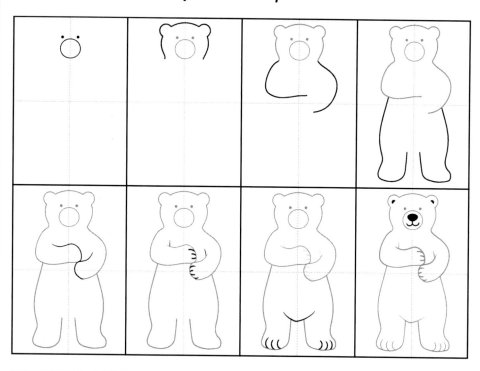

Unscramble the Keys!

The Beefeaters have got their keys in a muddle.
Can you help them find the right keys for each lock?
Label each lock with the correct keys.

KEY: _____

KEY: _____

KEY: _____

Six ravens always live at the Tower. It's said that if they ever leave, the kingdom will fall!

The Tower holds the Crown Jewels, the nation's most precious treasures. It includes the world's biggest diamond, the Cullinan I, in the Sovereign's Sceptre.

TOWER OF LONDON

The Tower of London has been home to exotic animals, like lions, elephants, and even a polar bear. Most were given as gifts to the Kings and Queens.

Officially called 'His Majesty's Royal Palace and Fortress of the Tower of London', it's over 900 years old. In that time, it's been a royal palace, a prison, a zoo, and even a mint where coins were made.
The Tower's Guards are called Yeoman Warders, but people call them Beefeaters. They live within the castle walls with their families.
The Ceremony of The Keys is the historic tradition of locking the Tower gates. It has taken place every single day for over 700 years.

TOWER BRIDGE

The walkways between the towers have glass floors, so you can look down on the road and river below!

The original colour of the bridge wasn't blue, but chocolate brown, thought to be Queen Victoria's favourite colour.

Tower Bridge is named after its neighbour, the Tower of London. Although its stone structure looks similar to the Tower, the bridge is actually 800 years younger, built in 1894. Around 31 million bricks were used to make the bridge. Tower Bridge is a 'bascule' bridge, meaning it can lift up in the middle, letting big boats pass underneath. In December 1952, a London bus was forced to jump the gap after the bridge began to rise. The bridge watchman had forgotten to ring the bell to warn people!

Make the Leap!

Draw your own London bus making the amazing leap across the gap in Tower Bridge!

Can you find 5 hidden buses on this page?

Floating in the Thames near Tower Bridge is an old war ship called HMS Belfast. It was first used during the Second World War. Its guns were so powerful, they cracked the ship's toilets when they fired. The ship is nearly as long as two Big Bens lying end-to-end.

A POSTCARD FROM LONDON

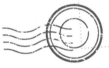

POSTCARD

Scan Me For Activity Solutions